not this
not that

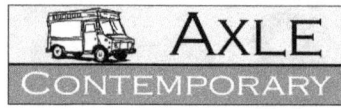

Published by
Axle Contemporary Press
P.O. Box 22095
Santa Fe NM 87502
www.axlepress.com

ISBN 978-0-9963991-0-4

references, precedents, and discussion at notthisnotthat2015.com

not this
not that

an exhibition catalogue

Axle Contemporary
may 29 - june 7
2015